Ladybirds

Natural pest control

**Ladybird gardening for beginners:
the natural history of these useful
insects and how to encourage them**

Darren J. Mann

Osmia **Publications, Banbury**

First published in 2002 by *Osmia* Publications, Banbury, UK

© *Osmia* Publications 2002

ISBN 0-9539906-6-4

A CIP record for this title is available from the British Library.

Cover Photograph: Seven spot ladybird *Coccinella 7-punctata* : A group of the seven spot ladybirds feeding on aphids.
© Ken Preston-Mafham, Premaphotos Wildlife

Production by *Osmia* Publications

Designed by Louisa Stevens

Printed and bound in Thailand by Gift Export Co. Ltd

About the Author

Darren J. Mann works in the Hope Entomological Collections of the Oxford University Museum Of Natural History. Here, he is in charge of the extensive beetle collections and the displays of live insects.

Beetles have been a passion in Darren's life for more than ten years and his specialist research interests are centred on the taxonomy (classification) of dung beetles and flower-visiting chafers. He also has an interest in cockroaches and is generally interested in, and is a recognised expert on, the principles of insect collection management.

Darren's research interests have taken him to the foothills of the Himalayas, the Namib Desert of Namibia and the rice paddies of The Gambia.

Acknowledgements

I would like to thank Terry Denman and Adam Wright who first taught me entomology, and George McGavin who continues to do so. I would also like to thank Max Barclay, John Deeming, Chris O'Toole, Steve Lane and John Ismay whose enthusiasm, knowledge and discussions about entomology keep me focused.

Contents

COLOUR PLATES

Plate 1

Lifecycle of the seven spot ladybird, *Coccinella 7-punctata* - stage 1, *Adults mating: A pair of seven spot lady-birds copulating on a nettle leaf.* © *Ken Preston-Mafham, Premaphotos Wildlife*

Plate 2

Lifecycle of the seven spot ladybird, *Coccinella 7-punctata* - stage 2, *Ova: The eggs of most species are laid on the underside of a suitable aphid bearing plant.* © *Ken Preston-Mafham, Premaphotos Wildlife*

Plate 3

Lifecycle of the seven spot ladybird, *Coccinella 7-punctata* - stage 3, *Larvae: The characteristically shaped larvae. This individual is munching away on its aphid meal.* © *Ken Preston-Mafham, Premaphotos Wildlife*

Plate 4

Lifecycle of the seven spot ladybird, *Coccinella 7-punctata* - stage 4, *Pupae: The typical domed pupae of the seven spot ladybird.* © *Ken Preston-Mafham, Premaphotos Wildlife*

Plate 5

Ladybird pupae: The pupae of some ladybirds remains in the last larval skin, such as the kidney-spot ladybird Chilocoris renipustulatus. *The larvae (to the right) of this ladybird has characteristic "spikes".*
© *Ken Preston-Mafham, Premaphotos Wildlife*

Plate 6

Two spot ladybird Adalia 2-punctata: *A mating pair. The male on top is one of the many colour varieties of this species. The female below is the more typical form.* © *Ken Preston-Mafham, Premaphotos Wildlife*

Plate 7

Seven spot ladybird Coccinella 7-punctata : *A group of the seven spot ladybirds feeding on aphids.*
© *Ken Preston-Mafham, Premaphotos Wildlife*

Plate 8

The ten spot ladybird has many colour varieties. This mating pair are of the more typical form. Note the distinctive pronotal patterning. © *Ken Preston-Mafham, Premaphotos Wildlife*

Plate 9

A colour variety of the ten spot, where the middle spots form a continuous zig-zag band.
© *Ken Preston-Mafham, Premaphotos Wildlife*

Plate 10

The fourteen spot ladybird, Propylea 14-punctata *is one of only a few British "spotted" ladybirds that is yellow. This is a common species of nettle beds.* © *Ken Preston-Mafham, Premaphotos Wildlife*

Plate 11

The pine ladybird, Exochomus quadripustulatus *is predominantly a tree dweller and as here often seen running about on the trunks of trees. This species is particularly common in cities on trees with Horse-chestnut scale.*
© *Richard A. Jones*

Plate 12

The Bryony ladybird Epilachna argus: *This distinctive species is one of only two vegetarian ladybirds in Britain. The size and colour of this introduced species make it unmistakeable.* © *Richard A. Jones*

Plate 13

Ladybird killer: This seven spot ladybird, Coccinella 7-punctata *has been attacked, paralysed and eaten from within. The cocoon containing the developing adult braconid wasp* Dinocampus coccinellae *is clearly visable underneath the ladybird.* © *Ken Preston-Mafham, Premaphotos Wildlife*

Plate 14

The twenty-four spot ladybird, Subcoccinella 24-punctata *is Britain's only native vegetarian ladybird. Luckily it's generally not interested in garden plants. A common species of meadows, where it feeds on herbaceous plants.*
© *Richard A. Jones*

Plate 15

The eyed ladybird, Anatis ocellata *is Britain's largest native species. The black marks on the elytra are often encircled by pale cream-yellow, hence the common name. Although widespread in Britain, this species prefers conifer woods where it feeds on aphids.* © *Richard A. Jones*

Plate 16

An OBC Ladybird House

ONE

"Ladybird, Ladybird, fly away home..."

We have all heard the saying and we all know the insect: ladybirds are one of the most popular insect groups, rightly regarded as the gardener's friend, of no threat to people and always perceived as the good guys in the media and literature. The common name prefix "lady-" is believed to be a dedication to the Virgin Mary, Our Lady. It is thought, to have been first applied to the seven spot ladybird, with the red representing her cloak in which she is often depicted and the seven spots representing the seven joys and seven sorrows of The Virgin. In fact, of the three hundred or so common names applied to this group of insects around the world, almost one quarter are in some way dedicated to The Virgin Mary. Ladybirds, sometimes called lady beetles or ladybugs, are all members of the beetle family Coccinellidae.

Ladybirds, along with all other insects, are an integral part of the ecosystem, ensuring that nutrients are recycled, flowers are pollinated and pests are kept in check. As well as being a source of natural pest control, ladybirds add both colour and enjoyment to the garden.

What is a Ladybird?

Ladybirds being insects have six legs and three main body parts, the head, thorax and abdomen. All ladybirds belong to the order of insects called the Coleoptera commonly known as beetles, which also includes the well known stag beetle (*Lucanus cervus*), the maybug or cockchafer (*Melolontha melolontha*) and the devils' coach horse (*Staphylinus olens*). The Coleoptera is the largest order of insects and is even the biggest group of organisms on the planet: with some 370,000 species, they constitute over 37% of the known insect species. Beetles range in size from 0.1mm to 180mm in length, though most are around 25mm long; they occur in every part of the world except the extremes of the Polar Regions. In Britain, the beetles are third largest order of insects with over 4,500 species.

The name Coleoptera is derived from the Greek *coleos* meaning sheath and *pteron* meaning wing, thus sheath winged insects, the name referring to the hard front wing cases (elytra) of beetles. These elytra, which meet in the centre-line of the body, together with chewing mouthparts, distinguish the Coleoptera from most of the other insect orders. The only group of insects likely to be confused with the Coleoptera are the true bugs (Order Hemiptera), which also include both important pest and beneficial insects. However, true bugs can be separated from beetles by the way the wings overlap, so do not meet in the midline, and the fact that all bugs have needle-like 'sucking' mouthparts.

The ladybirds belong to a family of beetles called the Coccinellidae, which includes some 5,200 species world-wide and range in size from just 0.8mm to over 10mm. Most coccinellids look like the typical ladybirds we know, in being patterned with red and black or yellow and black, but this is not always the case: a large number of the smaller species are uniformly coloured and hairy (pubescent), although these smaller coccinellids are generally not referred to as true ladybirds.

As the true ladybirds are so popular, they are one of the only groups of beetles where the majority of the species have been given common or vernacular names. Most of these are descriptive, based on the various colour patterns on the elytra. In Britain we have the two, five, seven, ten, fourteen, sixteen, twenty-two and twenty-four spot ladybirds, names which are merely based on the number of spots. However, there is also the eyed, kidney-spot and cream-spot, where the names describe the shape or colour of the spots themselves, several species are given names based on their habitat preference, such as the water ladybird and the heather ladybird. Similarly in America common names are given to a number of species, though in some cases with more imagination than we seem to have used. American species include the convergent, ashy grey, variable, spotted and my personal favourites, the twice-stabbed lady beetle and the mealybug destroyer.

The coccinellids are correctly identified as such by a number of characters, but the basics are:

- Oval-oblong domed body.
- Short antennae (8-11 segments), with a terminal 3 segmented club.
- Spatulate maxillary palps.
- Head partly to completely hidden from above.
- Legs are short and retractable under the body, where they sit in grooves.
- Four segmented tarsi (feet), which appear to be only three segmented due to the tiny third segment which is hidden inside the lobed second segment (known as pseudotrimerous tarsi) .

The Coccinellidae comprise eight subfamilies. The majority of the world ladybirds are predators of mites, scale insects, whitefly, aphids and other small invertebrates. However, the members of the subfamily Epilachninae are plant feeders (phytophagous). One member of this subfamily, the Mexican bean beetle (*Epilachna varivestis*) which feeds on members of the bean family (Fabaceae) is a serious pest in parts of America. Members of the Psylloborini (part of the subfamily Coccinellinae) feed exclusively on fungal growths (mildews).

About fifty species of coccinellids have been recorded occurring in Britain (appendix 1), although of these only about forty-two are native, and two are established aliens. About one dozen British species are listed in the national *Red Data Book* of threatened species. In other words, nearly one quarter of our ladybirds are in decline and in need of conservation. Furthermore, three species are now thought to be extinct, such as the thirteen spot ladybird (*Hippodomia* 13-*punctata*)*,* which was last recorded in Sussex during 1952. However, we have also gained a few species in the last decade. For example, the small ladybird *Rhyzobius chrysomeloides*, which was first reported as breeding in Britain during 1999 has now spread to numerous localities in the south-east of England.

Ladybirds are found throughout the British Isles and in most habitats, although there are some species that may be restricted to a particular habitat or to a particular part of the country. For example, the water ladybird (*Anisosticta* 19-*punctata*) is nearly always found at the edges of water on reeds and reedmace plants, the scarce seven spot ladybird (*Coccinella magnifica*) is only found near the nests of wood ants (*Formica rufa*) and the five spot ladybird (*Coccinella* 5-*punctata*) is only found in a few counties in Wales and Scotland where it is associated with river shingle. The majority of our species are predatory on aphids, white fly, scale insects and other soft-bodied invertebrates, although we have two plant feeders (bryony & twenty-four spot ladybird), and three mildew feeders (sixteen-spot, twenty-two spot & orange ladybird).

TWO

Life History

Like all other beetles, ladybirds have four stages to their life history:

egg (ova) • larva • pupa • adult (imago)

This life history strategy is known as complete metamorphosis (or holome-tabolous), with the larva being equivalent to the caterpillar stage of butterflies and moths and the pupa being equivalent to the chrysalis. The larval stage is one of active feeding. During the pupal stage, larval tissues are broken down and re-assembled into adult structures. This contrasts with the insects that go through an incomplete metamorphosis (hemimetabolous), such as true bugs (e.g. aphids) and grasshoppers. Here, there is no pupal stage and the larvae, often called nymphs, resemble miniature versions of the adults which moult their skins sev-eral times as they grow in size. In these insects, the wings appear as pads in the later stages and eventually reach full size in the final, adult stage.

After mating, the female lays the eggs on a suitable plant, usually one with an abundant source of food (e.g. aphids). These eggs are generally elongate and often yellowish in colour (resembling small yellow rice grains). The eggs are laid in batches of between 20-40 eggs; a single female ladybird can lay up to 1,500 eggs in her lifetime. The number of eggs per batch and the number of eggs laid per female varies between species and is also dependant the quality and abun-dance of the food available to the female. In some species the eggs are pro-tected by secretions produced the female; this is thought to help deter parasi-toids and even cannibalism, which may be quite common when food is scarce.

The larvae emerge around four days after the eggs are laid. However, the timing of this, along with all stages of development, is temperature dependent. The larva moults its skin several times as it grows; the stage between hatching from the egg and between each moult is called an instar. Immediately after hatching, the first instar larva eats the empty eggshell, and then wanders off in search of its first aphid meal. In those species that feed on aphids (see appendix 1), the tiny first instar larva often rides 'piggy-back' on the aphid, which is mas-sive by comparison. Ladybird larvae are grub-like in appearance and, according to species, are slate grey, to brown in colour and are often marked with spots of black, yellow or white. In some species, such as those of of *Scymnus* and *Cryp-tolaemus,* the larvae produce a waxy secretion for protection and almost look like mealy bugs. They have six short, stout legs, and taper towards the back (plate

3). The larva shed their skin three times, increasing in size after each moult. The time between moults depends on both temperature and food availability, but on average, larval development takes between 10 to 35 days.

At the end of the last instar, the full-grown larva stops feeding and prepares to pupate. The pupae of the Coccinellidae are not protected by a cocoon, as in some other beetle groups and so the larvae often wander some distance from the feeding area to avoid being eaten at this vulnerable stage. Once a suitable location has been found the larva attaches itself to the substrate, adopting a characteristic hunched position; the larval skin then splits, revealing the pupa. (plate 4)

The pupa in most ladybirds looks like a hunched-up larva, but without visible appendages. The colour of pupae varies with species and can even be affected by environmental conditions, but is usually similar to that of larvae. Although the pupa may seem immobile, it does have an alarm reaction if irritated. This is stimulated through a tactile response, and is thought to be a parasitoid evasion system: the pupa raises itself up and down and flicks away any attacking parasitoids (mostly tiny wasps). There is variation within species as to the strength of this response and it is even absent in the pupae of some species.

After about two weeks, the adult emerges through a split in the front end of the pupa. This process involves contractions of the abdominal muscles and may take up to several minutes. The newly emerged adult is a pale yellow-orange and lacks all the typical colour and spots. The cuticle or exoskeleton at this point is also very soft, and it may take several hours to harden up. During this time, blood (haemolymph) is pumped throughout the hindwings and elytra to inflate them. Eventually the cuticle hardens and at the same time, the final adult colour pattern is established. Once this is achieved, the ladybird begins to feed, then, after several weeks of building up food reserves in the body, it will find a place to hibernate. Ladybirds usually start to look for hibernation sites during September and October; this is one of most critical parts of the ladybirds' year, because a poor choice of hibernation site could lead to death. Some species are very fussy in making this choice and have specific sites in which to pass the winter, whilst others, such as the seven spot ladybird (*Coccinella 7-punctata*), have catholic tastes and will hibernate under loose bark, in grass tussocks and in outbuildings. Some species hibernate gregariously and aggregations of up to several thousand may congregate in one site. It is thought that there a pheromonal marking scent indicates these hibernation sites. In some localities in America and Turkestan, piles of dead ladybirds inches thick have been found on occasion, suggesting that these sites had been used for several years; at one site an entomologist estimated that there were ten thousand ladybirds per square foot!

Ladybirds become active as soon as the warmer weather of spring arrives and, in the case of predatory species, when the aphids have emerged. This generally takes place in March, although those species that feed on conifer feeding insects usually emerge earlier with their hosts.

Feeding is the first item on a ladybird's agenda after hibernation. Then searching for a mate is the next priority. In ladybirds there appears to be no long distance pheromonal attraction between mates; it seems that they rely on chance encounters, and probably short distance visual stimuli. As a rule, a male, on meeting another ladybird, will clamber onto its back, irrespective of its sex. If the mounted beetle turns out to be another male, the coupling is quickly broken off. It is not certain whether this is because the males recognise each other as being of the wrong sex or if it is due to the lack of specific female pheromone.

Mating behaviour in ladybirds is simple, and in general, copulation takes place soon after the initial encounter, although a female will reject males if she is hungry or recently mated.

Copulation lasts from one to eight hours; in some species repeated mating is needed to ensure high levels of fertility.

Unfortunately, copulation isn't without a certain amount of risk: the parasitic mite *Coccipolipus hippodaminae* (Acarina: Popadolipidae), which is usually found on the two-spot ladybird, is almost the equivalent of the human crab louse (*Phthirus pubis*), and, like it, is transmitted venereally. Although, unlike the human crab louse, this sexually transmitted parasite causes infertility.

THREE

Enemies of ladybirds

There has been very little research on the diseases, predators, parasites and parasitoids of ladybirds in Britain. A parasitoid is an insect that develops within or on the host, eventually causing its death. The disease agents include protozoans, pathogenic fungi and bacteria, all of which can be fatal. Of these the biggest killers of ladybirds are probably fungi such as *Beauveria* species. Over-wintering ladybirds are very susceptible to this pathogen,   especially those that hibernate gregariously; presumably this is aggregations make it easier for the fungus to spread *en masse*.

The bacterial parasite *Wolbachia*, attacks worms and insects all over the globe, in some cases turning infected males into females! In ladybirds, the infected male eggs die before they have chance to develop. The hatching female larvae then feast on this free meal, thus becoming infected with the bacteria. In some ladybird populations this gives rise to unequal sex ratios.

When attacked by a predator such as ants, a ladybird will try either to fly away or clamp down on the substrate, thus protecting its vulnerable underside. If the substrate is uneven, and the ladybird is unable to produce a predator proof seal against it, then it will angle its body towards the attacker, thus deflecting the attack from its underside. This defensive posture will usually protect the ladybird from say, a single ant, though, if there is a group of ants, the ladybird often loses.

The yellow/red/black markings of ladybirds are warning colours, which signal to would-be predators that these insects are distasteful. The defensive secretions produced by ladybirds belong to a group of chemicals called alkaloids. These chemicals are synthesised internally by the ladybirds, although some other defensive chemicals can be sequestered by the intake of poisonous foods. When a ladybird is attacked, it releases these chemicals from the 'knees', a process known as reflex bleeding. This 'blood' is itself brightly coloured, usually yellow or orange and has been shown to be distasteful to birds and lizards. It probably helps protect the ladybirds from all manner of predators and parasitoids, yet despite this protection, spiders and ants are undeterred and eat ladybirds with impunity.

Mimicry of the warning colours of ladybirds is quite common by other insects which are themselves not chemically protected. It occurs in insects such as fungus beetles (Endomychidae), leaf beetles (Chrysomelidae), true bugs (e.g. shieldbugs: Pentatomidae) and even in some Philippine cockroaches (Blattellidae).

In Britain a number of organisms parasitize ladybirds. They include two genera of flies (Diptera: Tachinidae & Phoridae), six genera of parasitic wasps (Hymenoptera: Braconidae & Chalcidoidea), one genus of mite (Acarina) and three genera of roundworm (Nematodea). The biologies of these vary: one chalcid wasp (*Homalotylus* sp.) is a gregarious internal parasitoid of ladybird larvae, while the larvae of the tachinid fly (*Degeeria luctuosa*) attack the immobile prepupa. The mite, *Coccipolipus hippodaminae,* already mentioned, is sexually transmitted and piggybacks under the elytra of the adult ladybird, sucking its haemolymph.

One of the most specialised and well-studied parasitoids is the tiny braconid wasp *Dinocampus coccinellae,* which is also by far the most studied. Its life-cycle is reminiscent of the monster in the film *Aliens.* This small wasp is parthenogentic, which means it produces viable eggs without having to mate, producing only female offspring. The female wasp has an everted egg-laying tube or ovipositor protruding from the end of its abdomen. It chases an adult ladybird with its ovipositor thrust forward, and, once contact is made, inserts the ovipositor through any weak spot in the exoskeleton, rather like a hypodermic syringe and injects eggs into the ladybird's body cavity.

The eggs hatch within five days, and the first instar larvae, which have large grasping mandibles, fight to the death until only one survives. This is because a ladybird can support the development of only one wasp to adulthood. This solitary larva then begins to feed on the host, avoiding all the essential organs, so that the ladybird does not die immediately. The ladybird becomes immobile just before the full-grown wasp larva is ready to leave; it emerges from the membranes between the plates of the beetle's abdomen. Once emerged, the larva begins to spin a cocoon on the underside between the legs of the ladybird, which is still partially paralysed (plate 13). Because the ladybird is still alive, both the warning colours and the defensive secretions are in operation, thus protecting the wasp while it pupates. Eventually, though, the ladybird will die either from starvation or fungal infection.

Unfortunately, not all of the dangers that ladybirds face are natural. As already mentioned some of our species are currently under threat, and although we do not completely understand the causes of their decline, the loss of habitat though development, agricultural intensification and the use of broad-spectrum insecticides, are major contributing factors. Some recent studies have even shown that the use of genetically engineered crops has a detrimental effect on ladybirds. In one study, ladybirds that were fed on aphids that had been reared on transgenic insect resistant crops showed a dramatic decline in fertility, egg hatching rate and premature death of the adults.

FOUR

Ladybird Solutions to the Pest Problem

A pest can be any organism that has a deleterious effect upon our crops, garden plants or even livestock; it is a purely anthropomorphic term for any organism that is in the wrong place at the wrong time and in the wrong numbers. Most of these so-called pests have an important role within the natural ecosystem, whatever their damaging activities on our plants and livestock.

The majority of us are indoctrinated to think that pest control must involve spraying insecticides on our plants: often at the first sign of a 'bug', which may or may not actually be a cause for concern. The first thing before doing anything else is to find out what 'bugs' are on your plants, are they friend or foe? This can be achieved through the numerous gardening books, insect guides and garden pest guides such as those by Chinery (1986), McGavin (2000 & 2001) and Savigear (1992). If you completely fail on your own, or just need help, it is generally possible to get advice from horticultural societies, who usually offer pest identification services to their members. However, it is not necessary to identify the 'bug' to species level, with a complete scientific name, but it is important to "know thine enemy!" Once the 'bug' is identified as a pest, you can begin to think about what action to take. The identification of the pest species allows for a better understanding of that pest and controls necessary: it is often possible to target your control in a more effective way when you know more about the biology and ecology of the pest involved.

The insecticidal bombardment of pests may be cost effective in the short term, but with growing concerns of the effects these chemicals have on both the environment and on our health, alternative methods are being sought. Moreover, there are additional problems as more and more pest species develop strains which are resistant to certain insecticides. With the ever-increasing restrictions on 'home-use' insecticides, cultural and biological control methods are becoming more important in the never-ending battle against pests in the garden.

Cultural control is the most basic of all pest control methods; and has been employed by humans since the beginning of crop cultivation. This predominantly involves crop rotation, handpicking pests off plants and general garden sanitation. Crop rotation simply means changing the type of plant at a particular location within your garden. This often happens on a three-year rotation, although in smaller gardens this should be prolonged. Since some species of pest occur in the soil at the base of their host plant, if the plant is removed the pest cannot survive. Alternatively, but less effectively, the plant can be simply dug into the ground. This method will also help enrich the soil, through the recycling of nutri-ents via breakdown of the plant material in the soil. The handpicking of pests is well known, especially for larger pests such as caterpillars or slugs. Using a spray or jet of water, often with a detergent (e.g. washing-up liquid) can be used for smaller pests such as aphids and whitefly. Garden sanitation, such as the removal of post-harvest crop remains, diseased or infested plant material, all help to eliminate the hiding places for pests and any individuals remaining on the plants.

Biological Control: this is the use by humans of a predator or parasitoid to control the numbers of another organism, namely the pest. The use of biological control agents and **Cultural Control** as part of **Integrated Pest Management (IPM)** strategies are becoming increasingly popular with both commercial produc-ers and the horticulturist. In fact, the first, and probably the most successful bio-logical control programme involved a ladybird. In 1887 the citrus crops in Califor-nia, USA, were under attack from the cottony cushion scale (*Icerya purchasi*), which had been introduced from Australia. The Vedalia ladybird (*Rodalia cardi-nalis*), a natural predator of this scale in Australia, was introduced over the next few years, and by 1890 a three-fold increase in the harvest was noticed and the Californian citrus industry was saved.

In our gardens, there is already a complete army of predators and parasi-toids, which, with a little encouragement, can help to keep most pests under con-trol, and, as part of an IPM scheme, reduce the need for insecticidal treatments. Natural control agents are numerous, and include microbes (such as bacteria), nematode worms (which are not used for aphid control), and parasitoids (such as braconid wasps and chalcid wasps) and predators (such as hoverflies, lacewings and of course, ladybirds).

Biological control can be broken down into three types: **Manipulative, Aug-mentative and Inoculative. Manipulative biological control** is the most basic, and simply capitalises on the beneficial insects already present in the garden. All that is done is that conditions are made more favourable for these insects, such as the avoidance of insecticidal treatments and 'friendly' gardening practices are undertaken.

Augmentative biological control is adopted when the ladybirds already present in the garden are unable to control the pests to the required level; they are supplemented with more ladybirds. These are artificially introduced, either through purchase from commercial dealers or from 'in-house' captive breeding.

Inoculative biological control involves the release of ladybirds (or other biocontrol agents) into an area in which they are not already present. This method is used when a new pest is introduced into a country or area, and is gen-erally not that useful to the home gardener, at least until widely tested by the proper authorities elsewhere. The case of the Vedalia ladybird used against cottony cushion scale in California is the classical example of this type of biological control.

One of the most common and important group of pests on plants are the aphids, also called greenfly or blackfly, of which there are around 500 species in Britain. As well as reducing the health of the plant by 'sucking' the sap, aphids excrete excess sap as sweet, sticky honeydew onto the foliage and this encourages the growth of moulds and sooty fungus. Moreover, when aphids insert their sucking mouthparts into plant tissues, they often introduce viral and fungal diseases which reduce plant fertility and productivity. Aphids are masters of survival. For example, in an optimal growing season, a single female cabbage aphid has the potential to produce 1,560,000,000,000,000,000,000,000,000 more aphids. Thankfully, through disease, predation, food availability, competition, and climate, this never happens. The aphids are probably the most serious pests to the horticulturist, though, luckily, nature has provided us with the perfect killing machine: the ladybird.

FIVE

Garden Ladybirds: Species Portraits

Most gardens already have ladybirds, and usually more than one species. Some of these will be small, unobtrusive and go unnoticed, others will be more obvious, as they go about their business of aphid hunting. The identification of the larger 'spotted' ladybirds is relatively easy, especially with the excellent *Naturalists' Handbook* on Ladybirds by Michael Majerus and Peter Kearns. This book includes a wealth of information, identification keys to most of the British species and coloured plates of the British ladybird fauna and is thoroughly recommended. *The Ladybirds of Surrey* by Roger Hawkins, is another excellent book, and also contains a mass of information on the ladybirds for that county and includes superb colour photos of ladybirds in their natural surroundings. For those of you who wish to learn just about everything known concerning these interesting insects *The Ladybirds*, in the New Naturalist Series, written by the leading British ladybird expert, Michael Majerus. is the one-stop reference guide.

The two-spot ladybird (*Adalia 2-punctata*) (plate 6)
The two-spot ladybird is often referred to as the 'gardeners friend', as it has a particular liking for aphids on roses. It is the probably the most frequently encountered species in inner city areas and, along with the seven spot ladybird, is universally recognised as 'the ladybird'. The genus *Adalia* has four central European species, of which two are found in Britain. The two-spot is one of the most widespread species of ladybirds in the world, being found throughout the northern hemisphere. It is found throughout Britain in most habitats, although rarely in grasslands, conifer plantations or at altitude.

This is a very variable species, but is generally red with a pair of black spot on the elytra, with a pair of white marks covering most of the side of the pronotum and a smaller pair centrally on the pronotal base. There are more than one hundred colour pattern varieties in this species. They vary from red with no spots, to black with two red spots and even to multi-spotted individuals.

The larvae are generally dark grey, with dark tubercles and with three spots in a triangular pattern, and, like those of the seven-spot, have been recorded feeding on aphids on a number of different host plants. This species hibernates in almost all situations, including exposed on trunks, in bark crevices, in leaf litter and plant debris. This is the most common species found hibernating indoors, where it often forms aggregations in the corner of windows and in doorframes or out buildings.

The two-spot ladybird is probably the most important of the garden ladybirds for the control of aphids and other soft bodied insects.

The ten-spot ladybird (*Adalia* 10-*punctata*) (plate 8 - 9)
This species occurs throughout the northern temperate zone of the old world (= Palaearctic Region), including China and Japan. It is an arboreal generalist and lives throughout Britain in most habitats, with a strong preference for woodland and hedgerow trees. Although rarely found on herbaceous plants, it appears to like certain crops (e.g. barley and wheat) and also nettles, probably because these plants tend to have high densities of aphids. Aggregations of the Chestnut Scale insect often attract this species, together with the Pine ladybird.

The ten-spot ladybird is one of the most variable of the British species, with various spot numbers and colour forms, ranging from completely black to almost completely red. The pronotum in the typical forms is pale with four black marks towards the base. It can be separated from most of the similar looking species by the fact it has pale legs. The larvae of this species resemble those of the two-spot ladybird in being grey, with three orange spots. However, they are generally darker in colour and some of the tubercles on the abdominal segments are pale. When conditions are favourable, this species can have a second generation in a single year.

Although it tends to hibernate close to the ground in leaf litter, plant debris and often in and around hedgerows, the ten-spot prefers to live in the upper parts of trees and bushes. If encouraged into the garden, however, this species, habitually a tree dweller, will feed on herbaceous plants with high aphid densities, and will help control aphids on ornamental and fruit trees.

The seven-spot ladybird (*Coccinella* 7-*punctata*) (plates 1 - 4, and 7)
The seven spot ladybird is one of the most recognisable of all the British insects. There are seven Central European species in the genus *Coccinella*, five of which occur in Britain; all are red or yellow with black spots. In Britain, the seven-spot is the most widespread and abundant. It occurs in all habitats, generally on low growing herbaceous plants.

This species is one of our largest native ladybirds, being up to 8mm in length; the elytra are red and have seven distinctive black spots, three on each side of the elytra and one large central spot at the base that often has a pair of white spots at either side. The thorax is black, with two large white marks at the front.

The larva is generally slate grey, with four pairs of yellow-orange spots and has been recorded feeding on aphids on more than 250 plant species. Hibernation sites are diverse, but usually at ground level, in plant litter and debris.

This is an important species in the garden for aphid control.

The fourteen-spot ladybird (*Propylea 14-punctata*) (plate 10)

One of the commonest central European ladybirds, in Britain this is probably the most widespread and abundant of all our ladybirds, being found in almost all habitats.

Unlike the other species mentioned so far, this species is creamy-yellow and black. The elytra have fourteen, often fused black squarish spots. The pronotum is yellow, with a large black mark which stretches half way towards the front.

The larvae of this species have a black ground colour with white spots, and have been recorded feeding on aphids on over 200 plant species. Although it appears to be only active for half the year, it often manages a second generation. The fourteen spot ladybird hibernates in most ground level sites, including plant debris, leaf litter, grass tussocks and hollow plant stems and sometimes in large groups.

Because it preys on a wide range of aphids on a wide range of plants, it is a very useful garden ladybird.

The pine ladybird (*Exochmus quadripustlatus*) (plate 11)

The Pine ladybird is becoming increasingly common in cities. Although predominantly associated with conifers, it has followed one of its foods into towns, the Chestnut Scale insect (*Pulvinaria regalis*). Accidentally introduced into Britain, this insect is now common on many city trees in the south, especially chestnut, sycamore and London plane. The adult female scales are about 5-8mm wide, brown, slightly convex and usually have large white powdery egg masses beneath them; they are most often found in the angles between branches and main stems. The larvae, pupae and adult ladybirds can often be seen amongst the scales insects and may well be keeping this alien pest under control.

The pine ladybird, along with its close relative the kidney-spot ladybird (*Chilocoris renipustalatus* with which it can be confused) is a tree dweller, being found on a number of conifer and deciduous trees, wherever scale insects are present. It is black, almost circular with a well defined lip around the edge (making it look almost like a World-War II German helmet), with four red marks on the elytra, the front pair comma shaped; the second pair, positioned just behind the middle, being more circular, in shape.

The larvae are light grey, with a pale central stripe and rows of dark grey, spiny tubercles. The centres of the tubercles are usually pale, giving the appearance of pale spots on the first abdominal segment. This species always pupates in the last larval skin (plate 5), usually *in situ* on the branches and trunks of trees in common with the kidney spot ladybird. Adults tend to hibernate in tree foliage, and in exposed bark crevices.

Although this species is not useful as a control agent of aphids on crop and ornamental herbaceous plants, it will help reduce scale insects, especially the horse-chestnut scale on trees and shrubs.

The bryony ladybird (*Epilachna argus*) (plate 12)
The bryony ladybird has only been established in Britain since 1997, but has subsequently turned up at a number of sites around the southern Home Counties, with a single specimen being found as far north as Coventry, in the West Midlands. This species is a native of southern Europe, and it is thought that it was accidentally introduced into this country on imported plants. It is one of the few herbivorous species

At 7mm long, the bryony ladybird is a large species; it has orange-red elytra with eleven, evenly spaced black spots and is covered with short downy hairs. The presence of these downy hairs makes it very easy to separate this species from all other large British ladybirds.

The larva is black and covered with branched spines. So far, it has not become a serious pest, being found mostly feeding on white bryony. However, this species is recorded from a number of other plants in the family Cucurbitaceae, which includes a number of crop plants such as cucumbers and courgettes.

The Australian ladybird (*Cryptolaemus montrouzieri*)
Originating in Australia, this ladybird has been widely distributed around the world for use in the biological control of mealy bugs. It was introduced to American citrus plantations in the late 1800s as a biocontrol agent and is known there as the mealybug destroyer. Although, our cold climate means that this species is unlikely to become common out-of-doors, it has recently been recorded surviving the winter at The Royal Horticultural Society's' Wisley Gardens, Surrey. The adults are unmistakable and unlikely to be confused with any British ladybird: they are 4mm in length and have black elytra, with an orange-red apex and are covered with short downy hairs, the head and the pronotum being orange red.

The larvae are covered with powdery white projections and resemble the mealy bugs on which they feed.

The Australian ladybird is used in Britain in glasshouses for the control of a variety of mealy bugs, such as the Citrus mealy bug (*Planococcus citri*) and some of the *Pseudococcus* species (Hemiptera: Pseudococcidae). In Britain it has been commercially available since the early 1980's and is widely used in botanical gardens and butterfly farms. Both the adults and the larvae feed on mealy bugs.

SIX

Other aphid predators in the garden

Aphids form an important food source for a number of other animals, from tiny flies to blue tits. Sympathetic gardening will allow these animals to thrive and help reduce the aphid problem as well as make the garden a more enjoyable place. The numerous spiders, earwigs, hoverflies, lacewings and flower bugs all devour their fair share of aphids. Some of these, such as the earwigs, may also have a detrimental effect, because they too can damage garden plants, but the majority of insects and other 'creepy-crawlies' in the garden are more beneficial than detrimental.

Flower bugs
Flower bugs are related to bed bugs and belong to the family Anthocoridae of the insect order Hemiptera (true bugs). Unlike the Diptera and the Coleoptera they go through an incomplete metamorphosis life cycle, which means they have no pupal stage. These small (3-5mm) bugs eat aphids by using their piercing mouthpart. Unfortunately, this group of bugs also has a tendency to bite people.

Hoverflies
The hoverflies belong to the family Syrphidae of the order Diptera (two-winged flies). There are about 250 species in Britain, of which about 100 have predacious larvae. The adults, which feed on nectar and honeydew, are often striped with yellow, orange and black and mimic wasps as a defensive strategy. However, unlike their wasp counterparts, they have no sting. It is the larvae of hoverflies that are avid predators of aphids. These are maggot-like, cylindrical and taper towards the head and reach up to 17mm in length. They mostly hide during the day in curled up parts of the plant or on the underside of leaves, coming out at night to feed.

Aphid midges
Aphid midges belong to the family Cecidomyiidae of the order Diptera. Most of the members of the family are gall formers and can themselves be pests. However, three species in Britain are predacious on aphids. These small flies (around 4mm in length) lay their eggs amongst aphid colonies, where the little orange larvae inject a paralysing venom into the aphids and then suck them dry.

Lacewings

The lacewings, as their names suggest, have a dense, lacy network of veins in their wings. They belong to the insect order Neuroptera, with the aphid predators in the families Chrysopidae and Hemerobiidae. As with the other non-ladybird aphid predators, the larvae eat the aphids, while the adults mostly feed on nectar, honeydew and pollen. The larvae have three pairs of legs and large jaws, somewhat similar in appearance to ladybird larvae. These larvae pierce the aphids with their jaws, injecting them with a mixture paralysing and digestive fluids, and then proceed to suck the prey dry.

SEVEN

Ladybird Friendly Gardening

If you have a garden, you will have ladybirds. However, the next step is to have enough ladybirds to help keep the numbers of pests down to acceptable levels. As previously mentioned, this example of **Manipulative Biological Control,** capitalizes on ladybirds already present by making the garden more favourable to them. There are a variety of ways by which this may be achieved, although success can never be guaranteed: when trying to manipulate nature in any way, there are no definitive answers, only guidelines as to the best practice.

First and foremost is the need to reduce the use of insecticides. Even in small doses, these chemicals will have a detrimental effect on ladybirds and other beneficial insects in the garden ecosystem. If pesticides are to be used as a last resort, then try to use those that are species-specific, which should, in theory, have little ill effect on non-target species. Alternatively, it may be possible to use commercially available treatments that introduce a fungal disease to the aphids. Generally, these fungal treatments are again species-specific. However, it is important to remember that if you eliminate your aphids, the aphid-dependant predators will also suffer. The loss of aphids from your garden plants can be compensated for by the use of aphid reservoirs (discussed below).

When possible the use of non-insecticidal control is preferable. This can be in the form of handpicking or brushing or the use of non-insecticidal sprays containing detergents. These detergent sprays will 'knock-off' aphids, with the detergent acting as an aphid irritant. This may also dislodge the ladybirds and other predators, but in general they are more robust than their aphid prey and so this process usually does not kill them, and eventually they will crawl back onto the plants, as will some of the aphids.

Wild patches: The concept of the 'wild-garden' is not new, although it is often associated with hippies, eccentrics, nature lovers or just plain lazy people. However, the value of such wild areas in the garden cannot be over-emphasised. The simple planting of small areas with so-called 'weeds' will be advantageous in a number of ways. Firstly, you will be creating suitable habitat for a large number of species, therefore increasing the overall biodiversity of your garden. Secondly, it will encourage and support beneficial insects in the following ways: the leaf litter and cover the plants provide will act as suitable over wintering sites for insects. The flowers and extrafloral nectaries will provide an alternative source of food. The planting of suitable plants that have high aphid densities will increase the overall ladybird yield each year and lastly, selected native plants can act as 'aphid reservoirs'.

Over wintering: The availability of hibernation sites for ladybirds is one of the most important factors in encouraging these insects into your garden. If each year the ladybirds have to leave your garden to find a place in which to spend the winter, they are unlikely to return the following year. Therefore, the provision of suitable 'nooks and crannies' in which these insects can hibernate is an essential part of ladybird friendly gardening.

Some species of ladybird form aggregations in winter, where, in a single area you may find from a couple of dozen to several hundred ladybirds; for example in the two-spot and the twenty-two spot ladybirds, aggregations of over one thousand have been known. This mass hibernating is probably pheromone driven. That is, when a good hibernation site is found, the insects will be use it year after year, the accumulation of pheromones produced by each year's inhabitants attracting more ladybirds. Since most ladybirds have an annual life cycle (i.e. live only one year), this pheromone must be long lasting since the new generation of ladybirds are attracted to the same locality. In some cases, these mass hibernation sites are occupied by more than one species, which suggests that this aggregation pheromone is not species specific. Unfortunately, as with so much other insect behaviour, we are far from understanding the finer details of the pheromone(s) and its effects. Artificial attractants, based on these aggregation pheromones, are becoming more widely available. The full impact that they may have on enticing ladybirds into your garden has not been tested over time, so experiment before you go the whole hog!

In collaboration with the Oxford Bee Company Ltd, I have designed a new and improved ladybird house. Made from environmentally friendly plastic, it comprises a box 20cm wide, 25cm high and 10cm deep. The front wall is in the form of a louvered door, which opens to reveal a honeycombed insulation material with lots of nooks and crannies in which ladybirds can spend the winter in frost-free hibernation. The door enables the gardener to see which species are using the ladybird house and also to gain access in spring to the interior in order to clean the roosting material of any dead insects and spiders which may have accumulated during winter. (See p. 32 for details of how to purchase ladybird houses.)

The location of ladybird houses is as important as their design. If all of your houses are attached to tree trunks, then you will provide a suitable over wintering site for some of the ladybird species that are potentially beneficial. However, to attract the full range of species, a number of the houses should additionally be placed at various localities around the garden in shady, ground level sites.

The provision of overwintering houses for ladybirds can enhance another and visually appealing measure to make gardens ladybird-friendly: growing suitable plants. Most garden ladybird species hibernate either on or near the ground in leaf litter, plant debris and hollow plant stems or will find suitable cracks and crevices on tree trunks, or merely sit in the foliage of evergreen trees. While many of these opportunities already exist in a typical garden, supplementary planting of native plants will, however, add to the appeal of your garden as wintering quarters for ladybirds.

Useful plants for the provision of hibernation sites include any perennial species that form basal rosettes, such as mulleins (*Verbascum* spp.) and evening primroses (*Oenothera* spp). Most plants that you can plant as aphid providers (nettles, thistles & umbellifers such as hogweed and fennel) will also provide suitable refugia for the ladybirds in the winter months. Any plants that have dense foliage, such as gorse, bramble, Scots pine and ivy (for tree dwellers) will all help to give a range of hibernation sites and pampas grass (*Cordateria selloana*), although not native, forms very suitable and substantial tussocks.

Aphid reservoirs

The garden needs to keep a continuous supply of aphids for those insects that are dependant on them. If at any time the cultivated plants cannot meet the demand for aphids by the predators, parasites and parasitoids, they will go elsewhere. A relatively straight forward solution to this, is to provide a source of non-pest aphids in your garden. This can be achieved through the planting of native plants, especially nettles and thistles. The species of aphids that occur on these two plants are more or less specific to them; there are of course exceptions to this. These native plants then act as 'aphid reservoirs', as they will keep a continuous supply of aphids in your garden. Nettles have the additional advantage in being food plants for caterpillars of attractive garden butterflies such as the Peacock (*Inachis io),* the Red Admiral (*Vanessa atalanta*) and the Small Tortoiseshell (*Aglais urticae*).

Alternative foods

Ladybird larvae and adults may supplement their normal aphid diet with other types of food, especially in times of prey scarcity. They will eat flower nectar, water and honeydew. Some plant species have nectar-secreting structures in various locations other than in the flowers. These are called extrafloral nectaries and produce nutrient rich secretions which insects seek out. The theory is that the plants use the extrafloral nectaries to attract predators and parasitoids for protection against herbivores such as aphids. It is important, therefore, that a range of flowers is available throughout the season; these can either be as part of your normal flower garden, or in the borders of vegetable plots. Plants such as vetches, thistles, hibiscus, passsiflora, buddleia, are all good food sources for ladybirds.

It is also possible to purchase 'ladybird feeders' through commercial garden outlets. These feeders resemble bird tables and are painted with bright colours, so as to look like flowers and therefore attract flower-visiting insects. They provide a platform on which to place a source of food, usually a sugar solution for the visiting insects. These feeders will attract a range of insects and not just ladybirds however and their effectiveness in Britain has not yet been thoroughly demonstrated.

Augmentative Biological Control

So far I have outlined the various ways in which we can encourage ladybirds to visit, breed and hopefully stay in our gardens. Unfortunately, this may not always be successful and so the artificial releasing of ladybirds into the garden is another ploy.. Obviously, if the garden is made suitable beforehand, as outlined above, then those ladybirds released are more likely to stay.

There are three ways of obtaining ladybirds:

Purchase: a number of commercial outlets deal in ladybirds and these can be found through your local garden centres or horticultural societies. When buying ladybirds, always buy from the beginning to mid-summer, because, by about September, the adults are more interested in finding a place in which to hibernate rather than eating your pest aphids. Secondly, always buy (if possible) larvae, because, unlike adults, they do not have option of flying away!

Pick-your-own ladybirds are simple and easy to come by: find some local waste-ground with suitable aphid ridden plants, such as nettles, umbellifers or thistles and pick off the ladybird larvae and adults. This practice may have repercussions in terms of depleting wild populations, so never remove all the ladybirds at any one locality and try not to visit the same site year after year. Of course you should always seek the landowners permission before harvesting their ladybirds!

Grow-your-own ladybirds (or captive breeding) is both profitable (in terms of beetle production or even selling to your neighbours!) and is much more enjoyable, even if there is a little more work involved. It can be used for educational purposes and may appeal to schools.

Some species of ladybird lend themselves to captive breeding indoors, which provides optimal conditions, away from predators, parasites, parasitoids and food shortages. Some of the easiest species to keep in this way are also the most beneficial to the garden, such as the two, seven and fourteen spot ladybirds.

The first step is to catch your ladybirds and provide them with a home. Suitable breeding containers include margarine tubs, jam jars and ice-cream containers. These must be cleaned of all grease and other contaminants because these may be detrimental to the ladybirds. The most practical types of cages are those that are easily cleaned and have easy access; Petri dishes make the best breeding containers. The base of the container should be covered in kitchen towel or other suitable moisture absorbent material. This prevents drowning, especially of small, young larvae

Sexing ladybirds is not an easy task, but on average females are larger. There are characters on the underside of the abdomen, but these require magnification. If you have access to a hand lens or a low powered dissecting microscope, then you can try and see these features. The males of most species (at least those we are interested in) have a tiny last abdominal segment, which has an indented basal margin, whereas in females, this segment is larger and the basal margin is not indented. Also, in general, the basal margins of the second to third visible abdominal segment in males has a curved band which differs from the remainder of the abdominal plate, for example glossy black in the two-spot, and yellowish in the fourteen-spot. Because of these sexing difficulties, it is often best to collect a number of specimens (of different sizes) to ensure you have both sexes. Alternatively, you can wild-collect egg batches, which are usually yellow in colour and laid on the underside of the leaves of aphid-laden plants, and rear the larva.

The most important thing in culturing ladybirds is to maintain a constant food supply, since ladybird larvae have cannibalistic tendencies in times of shortage. The easiest food is, of course, aphids, which can be wild caught, or even cultured themselves. Bean, pea and potato aphids are all easy to rear in pots on suitable host plants and if, kept in warm and light conditions, will often produce young all year round. However, since we are trying to reduce the aphid problem, breeding more seems a little self-defeating!

Live aphids are the best food and can be collected from the garden or nearby hedgerow plants, then placed in the rearing cages. Alternatively, you can collect live aphids into small plastic bags and then freeze them; this will not only help reduce your aphid problem but will also supply your ladybird cultures with food throughout the year. It is important to remember never to thaw and re-freeze the aphids because they will soon become mush. It is therefore advisable to remove only the required amount of aphids per-day. On average, a two-spot ladybird will eat about 10 a day, but remember the seven-spot is larger and will need up to three times as many aphids.

It is also possible to make artificial diets, based on yeast, liver, sugar and a few other ingredients. However, this beyond the scope of this text and the reader is referred to Majerus and Kearns (1989)- see Further Reading, p. 28

Once you have got your cage, your food supply and your ladybirds, the rest is easy! As soon as you have obtained eggs, it is best to remove the parent ladybirds, as they may make a meal of them. The eggs should be kept at room temperature and should hatch within seven days; any which do not hatch after that time and change colour are probably infertile and should be disposed of. The larvae will eat their empty eggshells on hatching and any un-hatched eggs they come across. They need a daily feed of live or recently thawed aphids; at first they will eat only a few, but, as they grow, so will their appetites. In about three weeks you should have your first crop of ladybird adults.

It is actually best to release nearly full-grown larvae rather than adults because they are more sedentary (i.e. they won't fly off over the fence!) and so will be more efficient at clearing plants of aphids.

In summary
- Reduction in insecticide use
- 'Natural' areas
- Hibernation sites
- Aphid reservoirs
- Provision of alternative foods
- Augmentative Biological Control

EIGHT

Frequently asked Questions

Can you age ladybirds by the number of spots?
The answer to this is No. The number of spots on an individual ladybird is related to the species to which that specimen belongs and not its age. The number of spots does vary between the different species and in those species that exhibit colour polymorphism; the number of spots may vary within the species or even a particular local population. Most ladybirds you will encounter will either has over-wintered from the previous year, having matured in late Summer, or be the product of the current year's breeding. You can use the number of spots, the general colour and size to identify a ladybird to species. In some species, such as the two-spot or the ten-spot ladybirds, the number of spots and the general colour of an individual may differ from the normal. For example, in the two-spot ladybird, more than one hundred different colour forms have been recognised. This species normally has a red ground colour and two distinct black spots; however, you can find specimens that are completely black with red spot, to specimens with no spots at all. This polymorphism results from genetic variation within the species.

Do ladybirds bite?
There are a few instances when ladybirds have been known to bite people. This usually occurs during population explosions, such as the 1976 Seven-Spot lady-bird 'plague', when a number of people were reportedly being bitten. Being bee-tles, ladybirds have chewing mouthparts, so they do have the ability to bite. How-ever, human flesh is unpalatable to ladybirds, and, on the occasions of people being bitten by ladybirds, it was probably by starving individuals checking people out as a potential source of food. Another possible explanation is that "biting" la-dybirds were in reality in need of salt during very hot weather and were trying to drink human sweat.

In general ladybirds will not bite, but if they do there is just a little pain and usually no side effects.

What should I do with ladybirds hibernating in my house?
Ladybirds hibernate in all manner of sites, from outhouse, garages, and porches and even behind the curtains in houses. Some species, such as the Two-Spot, can be found in buildings, sometimes in large groups. If the ambient temperature becomes high enough they may become active, and fly towards the light of a window. If you do find hibernating ladybirds, it is best to release them outside,

either on a warm day, or in a suitable frost free out house, such as a garage or shed, where they can spend the rest of winter without too much disturbance.

Further Reading

CHINERY, M. (1986) *Collins Guide to Insects of Britain and Western Europe.* Collins. 319pp.

HAWKINS, R.G. (2000) *Ladybirds of Surrey.* Surrey Wildlife Trust, Surrey. 136pp.

MAJERUS, M.E.N. (1994) *Ladybirds.* New Naturalist Series, 81. Harper Collins, London. 368pp.

MAJERUS, M. & KEARNS, P. (1989) *Ladybirds.* Naturalists' Handbook 10, Richmond Publishing Co. Ltd., Slough. 103pp.

MCGAVIN, G.C. (2000) Dorling Kindersley Handbooks: Insects, spiders and other terrestrial arthropods. Dorling Kindersley. 255pp.

MCGAVIN, G.C. (2001) Essential Entomology: an order by order introduction. Oxford University Press. 318pp.

ROTHERAY, G.E. (1989) *Aphid predators..* Naturalists' Handbook 11, Richmond Publishing Co. Ltd., Slough. 77pp.

SAVIGEAR, A. (1992) *Garden Pests and Predators: the wildlife in your garden and its ecological control.* Blandford, London.128pp.

Appendix 1

A List of the Ladybirds of the British Isles

Adapted from Majerus & Kearns, 1989, Majerus, 1994

Scientific Name	Common Name	Colour / Pattern	Status	Habitats	Distribution	Principle Food
Adalia 2-punctata	Two Spot Ladybird	Red, two black spots.	Resident, Common	Various	Widespread	Aphids
Adalia 10-punctata	Ten Spot Ladybird	Red, ten black spots, but highly variable.	Resident, Common	Woodlands, hedgerows	Widespread	Aphids
Anatis ocellata	Eyed Ladybird	Russet red, 18 black spots often ringed with cream	Resident, Common	Conifer woodland	Widespread	Aphids
Anisosticta 19-punctata	Water Ladybird	Buff, 19 black spots	Resident, Common	Wetlands	Widespread	Aphids
Aphidecta obliterata	Larch Ladybird	Pale tan-orange	Resident, Common	Conifer woodland	Widespread	Adelgids
Chilocoris renipustulatus	Kidney Spot Ladybird	Black, 2 red spots	Resident, Common	Woodland	Widespread	Coccids (scale insects)
Clitostethus arcuatus	Ladybird	Black yellowish horseshoe mark on elytra	Resident, Rare	Woodland	Southern England and Wales	Whitefly
Coccidula rufa	Ladybird	Reddish Brown	Resident, Common	Wetlands, on reeds	Widespread	Aphids
Coccidula scutellata	Ladybird	Reddish brown, with basal dark triangular mark on elytra	Resident, Local	Wetlands, on reeds	Widespread Southern England and Wales	Aphids

Scientific Name	Common Name	Colour / Pattern	Status	Habitats	Distribution	Principle Food
Coccinella 11-punctata	Eleven Spot Ladybird	Red, 11 black spots	Resident, Local	Generally costal, also found on industrial sites	Widespread	Aphids
Coccinella 5-punctata	Five Spot Ladybird	Red, five black spots	Resident, Rare	River shingle	South Wales and Scotland	Aphids
Coccinella 7-punctata	Seven Spot Ladybird	Red, seven black spots	Resident, Common	Various	Widespread	Aphids
Coccinella hieroglyphica	Hieroglyphic Ladybird	Brown, black stripes and spots	Resident, Common	Heathland	Widespread	Aphids
Coccinella magnifica	Scarce Seven Spot Ladybird	Red, seven black spots	Resident, Local	Woodland, usually near wood ants nests	Widespread	Aphids
Cryptolaemus montrouzieri	Australian Ladybird	Black, red-orange spots at apex of elytra, head and pronotum orange-red	Introduced as a Biological control agent	Greenhouses, recorded rarely out of doors.	Widespread	Coccids (scale insects)
Epilachna argus	Byrony Ladybird	Orange-red, 11 black spots	Introduced	Waste ground and Gardens	Southern England	Aphids
Exochomus 4-pustulatus	Pine Ladybird	Black, 4 red spots	Resident, Common	Conifer woodland	Widespread	Coccids (scale insects)
Exochomus 2-pustulatus	Heather Ladybird	Black, 6 red spots	Resident, Local	Heathland	Widespread	Coccids (scale insects)
Exochomus nigromaculatus	Ladybird	Black, bordered with yellow on pronotum	Resident, Rare	Heathland	England	Aphids

Scientific Name	Common Name	Colour / Pattern	Status	Habitats	Distribution	Principle Food
Halyzia 16-guttata	Orange ladybird	Orange, 12 or 16 creamy-white spots	Resident, Common	Woodland	Widespread	Mildews
Harmionia 4-punctata	Cream-streaked ladybird	Pink, salmon or brown, 14 or 16 black spots	Resident, Common	Conifer woodland	Widespread	Aphids
Hippodomia 13-punctata	Thirteen spot ladybird	Red, 13 black spots	Resident, thought Extinct	Marshland	East England	Aphids
Hippodomia variegata	Adonis Ladybird	Red, 7 black spots (variable)	Resident, Local	Various	Southern England Wales	Aphids
Hyperaspis pseudopustulata	Ladybird	Black, 4 black spots	Resident, Local	Predominantly Woodlands	Widespread, more common in the south	Aphids
Myrrha 18-guttata	Eighteen Spot ladybird	Maroon, 18 cream spots (variable)	Resident, Common	Conifer woodland	Widespread	Aphids
Myzia oblongoguttata	Striped ladybird	Chestnut, cream stripes and spots	Resident, Common	Conifer woodland	Widespread	Aphids
Nephus bisignatus	Ladybird	Black, pale border at rear end	Resident, Rare	Low growing vegetation	South east England	Coccids (scale insects)
Nephus quadrimaculatus	Ladybird	Black, 4 yellow spots	Resident, Rare	Grassland	Southern England	Coccids (scale insects)
Nephus redtenbacheri	Ladybird	Black, 2 orange spots	Resident, Common	Grasslands	Widespread	Coccids (scale insects)

Scientific Name	Common Name	Colour / Pattern	Status	Habitats	Distribution	Principle Food
Platynaspis luteorubra	Ladybird	Black, 4 orange-red spots	Resident, Local	Grasslands	Southern England and Wales, thought to be associated with the aphids in the nests of *Lasius* ants	Aphids
Propylea 14-punctata	Fourteen Spot ladybird	Yellow, 14 black spots	Resident, Common	Various	Widespread	Aphids
Psyllobora 22-punctata	Twenty-two Spot ladybird	Yellow, 22 black spots	Resident, Common	Meadowlands	Widespread	Mildews
Rhizobius chrysomeloides	Ladybird	Reddish	Introduced, Rare	Grasslands	Southern England spreading	Aphids
Rhizobius litura	Ladybird	Reddish-ochraceous, often with dark markings on elytra	Resident, common	Grasslands	Widespread	Aphids
Scymnus auritus	Ladybird	Black, thin pale border at rear of elytra	Resident, Common	Oak woodland	Widespread	Aphids
Scymnus femoralis	Ladybird	Black	Resident, Local	Grasslands	Widespread	Aphids
Scymnus frontalis	Ladybird	Black, 2 red spots	Resident, Local	Low growing vegetation	Widespread	Aphids
Scymnus haemorrhoidalis	Ladybird	Black, yellow-orange patch at tip of elytra	Resident, Common	Low growing vegetation	Widespread	Aphids
Scymnus limbatus	Ladybird	Red-brown, darker area centrally on elytra	Resident, Local	Woodland	Southern England	Aphids Coccids (scale insects)

Scientific Name	Common Name	Colour / Pattern	Status	Habitats	Distribution	Principle Food
Scymnus nigrinus	Ladybird	Black	Resident, Common	Conifer woodlands	Widespread, more common in the south	Aphids, Adelgids
Scymnus schmidti	Ladybird	Black	Resident, Local	Low growing vegetation	Widespread	Aphids
Scymnus suturalis	Ladybird	Red-brown, dark brown mark near base	Resident, Common	Conifer woodland,	Widespread	Aphids, Adelgids
Stethorus punctillum	Ladybird	Black	Resident, Local	Woodland	Widespread	Mites
Subcoccinella 24-punctata	Twenty-four Spot ladybird	Russet, 20 black spots	Resident, Common	Grassland and Meadows	Widespread	Plants
Tythaspis 16-punctata	Sixteen Spot ladybird	Creamy-buff, 16 spots (variable)	Resident, Common	Ground dwelling	Widespread	Coccids (scale insects) mildew
Vibidia 12-guttata	Twelve Spot ladybird	Orange, white spots	Resident, thought to be extinct	Woodland	Local	Mildews

Appendix 2

Where to get your ladybird houses

Ladybird houses, complete with full instructions, are available from the Oxford Bee Company Ltd:

The Oxford Bee Company Ltd.,
Ark Business Centre,
Gordon Road,
Loughborough,
LEICS
LE11 1JP

Tel: 01509 261654
Fax: 01509 643465
E-mail: info@oxbeeco.com
Website: http://www.oxbeeco.com

The Oxford Bee Company Ltd also supplies nest kits for the Red Mason Bee, *Osmia rufa,* the European Horned Mason Bee, *Osmia cornuta* and the European Blue Mason Bee, *Osmia coerulescens* as well as nests for bumblebees, *Bombus* spp.

For information leaflets and a complete price list of products supplied by the Oxford Bee Company Ltd and a list of publications distributed by the OBC, please contact the above.

The Oxford Bee Company Ltd. is a spinout company of Oxford University in conjunction with the University's Bee Systematics and Biology Unit and Isis Innovation Ltd., the University's technology transfer company.

Plate 1
Lifecycle of the seven spot ladybird, *Coccinella 7-punctata* - **stage 1**
Adults mating: A pair of seven spot ladybirds copulating on a nettle leaf.
© *Ken Preston-Mafham, Premaphotos Wildlife*

Plate 2
Lifecycle of the seven spot ladybird, *Coccinella 7-punctata* - **stage 2**
Ova: The eggs of most species are laid on the underside of a suitable aphid bearing plant.
© *Ken Preston-Mafham, Premaphotos Wildlife*

Plate 3
Lifecycle of the seven spot ladybird, *Coccinella 7-punctata* - stage 3
Larvae: The characteristically shaped larvae. This individual is munching away on its aphid meal.
© *Ken Preston-Mafham, Premaphotos Wildlife*

Plate 4
Lifecycle of the seven spot ladybird, *Coccinella 7-punctata* - stage 4
Pupae: The typical domed pupae of the seven spot ladybird.
© *Ken Preston-Mafham, Premaphotos Wildlife*

Plate 5

Ladybird pupae: The pupae of some ladybirds remains in the last larval skin, such as the kidney-spot ladybird Chilocoris renipustulatus. The larvae (to the right) of this ladybird has characteristic "spikes".
© Ken Preston-Mafham, Premaphotos Wildlife

Plate 6

Two spot ladybird Adalia 2-punctata: A mating pair. The male on top is one of the many colour varieties of this species. The female below is the more typical form.
© Ken Preston-Mafham, Premaphotos Wildlife

Plate 7
Seven spot ladybird Coccinella 7-punctata *: A group of the seven spot ladybirds feeding on aphids.*
© Ken Preston-Mafham, Premaphotos Wildlife

Plate 8
The ten spot ladybird, Adalia 10-punctata, *has many colour varieties. This mating pair are of the more typical form. Note the distinctive pronotal patterning.*
© Ken Preston-Mafham, Premaphotos Wildlife

Plate 9

A colour variety of the ten spot, Adalia 10-punctata, *where the middle spots form a continuous zig-zag band.*
© *Ken Preston-Mafham, Premaphotos Wildlife*

Plate 10

The fourteen spot ladybird, Propylea 14-punctata *is one of only a few British "spotted" ladybirds that is yellow. This is a common species of nettle beds.*
© *Ken Preston-Mafham, Premaphotos Wildlife*

Plate 11

The pine ladybird, Exochomus quadripus tulatus *is predominantly a tree dweller and as here often seen running about on the trunks of trees. This species is particularly common in cities on trees with Horse-chestnut scale.*
© *Richard A. Jones*

Plate 12

The Bryony ladybird Epilachna argus: *This distinctive species is one of only two vegetarian ladybirds in Britain. The size and colour of this introduced species make it unmistakeable.*
© *Richard A. Jones*

Plate 13

Ladybird killer: This seven spot ladybird, Coccinella 7-punctata *has been attacked, paralysed and eaten from within. The cocoon containing the developing adult braconid wasp* Dinocampus coccinellae *is clearly visable underneath the ladybird.*
© Ken Preston-Mafham, Premaphotos Wildlife

Plate 14

The twenty-four spot ladybird, Subcoccinella 24-punctata *is Britain's only native vegetarian ladybird. Luckily it's generally not interested in garden plants. A common species of meadows, where it feeds on herbaceous plants.*
© Richard A. Jones

Plate 15

The eyed ladybird, Anatis ocellata *is Britain's largest native species. The black marks on the elytra are often encircled by pale cream-yellow, hence the common name. Although widespread in Britain, this species prefers conifer woods where it feeds on aphids.*
© *Richard A. Jones*

Plate 16
An OBC Ladybird House